3 THINGS I WISH I'D KNOWN ABOUT PERSONAL FINANCE IN COLLAGE

PERSONAL FINANCE INSIGHT FOR A COLLAGE STUDENT

A.D RAMS

Contents

CHAPTER ONE 3

INTRODUCTION...3

The value of education in personal finance 4

The Value of Keeping a Budget and Monitoring Expenses 10

Knowing the fundamentals of creating a budget....................15

The advantages of planning for freedom and stability in finances 20

CHAPTER TWO 22

Establishing and Preserving Good Credit....................25

Definition of credit scores and why they matter 32

Putting Money Towards The Future 37

CHAPTER THREE 42

Investments and their long-term advantages.......................43

Investment choices that are appropriate for college students.47

The significance of knowing your risk tolerance and beginning to invest early...52

Comprehending Risk Tolerance 54

Summary 57

THE END 59

CHAPTER ONE

INTRODUCTION

Managing your own finances can be challenging, particularly if you're a college student trying to balance work, extracurricular activities, and school. Nonetheless, you can position yourself for long-term financial success and stability by learning the fundamentals of personal finance at a young age. We'll look at three important personal finance lessons that many people wish they had understood when they were in college in this post. During and after college, these insights can assist you in making well-informed decisions about money management, asset accumulation, and financial independence.

Whether you're just starting college or almost done, these insightful lessons will help you take charge of your financial future and make wise decisions that are consistent with your values and aspirations.

The value of education in personal finance

Education on personal finance is vital for people of all ages and backgrounds. Personal financial education is crucial for the following reasons:

Empowerment: By giving people the information and abilities necessary to make wise financial decisions, personal finance education enables people to take charge of their financial futures. Through comprehending ideas like debt management, investing, budgeting, and saving, people can successfully handle a variety of financial circumstances and reach their objectives.

The cornerstone of personal finance education is financial literacy, which includes knowledge and comprehension of financial ideas and principles. People can acquire the knowledge and abilities needed to properly manage their finances, steer clear of financial traps, and gradually accumulate wealth by fostering financial literacy through education.

Long-Term Financial Stability: Encouraging long-term financial security and stability requires a strong personal finance education program. People may create a strong financial foundation that supports their needs and aspirations now and in the future by learning how to budget, save, and invest properly. Furthermore, knowing responsible debt management techniques can avert future financial strain and adversity.

Goal Achievement: Whether a person is saving for a down payment on a house, financing an education, or making retirement plans, personal finance education assists them in identifying and achieving their financial objectives. People can work toward a better financial future and realize their dreams by learning how to develop practical financial plans and strategies.

Risk management: Reducing financial risk and guarding against unanticipated events require an understanding of financial concepts like insurance and estate planning. Those who have received personal finance education are better equipped to protect their financial future by making educated judgments regarding risk management techniques, estate planning, and insurance coverage.

Economic Stability: The general prosperity and stability of the economy are influenced by a financially literate populace. People are less likely to turn to government assistance programs or experience financial hardship when they have the information and abilities necessary to make wise financial decisions. Thus, the economy is strengthened and more opportunities for everyone to pursue the economy are created.

Decreased Financial hardship: People's mental and physical health can suffer greatly when they are under financial hardship. Education in personal finance enables people to handle their money more skillfully, which lowers financial stress and enhances general wellbeing. People might feel more financially secure and at ease by learning how to manage their debt, make and follow a budget, and make future plans.

Empathy and Understanding: Learning about personal finance helps people develop empathy and understanding for people from a range of socioeconomic backgrounds. People can have a deeper understanding of the significance of financial education and advocacy, which can result in more inclusive and equitable financial systems, by learning about financial difficulties and discrepancies.

personal finance education is critical for enabling people to make well-informed financial decisions, encouraging long-term security and stability, helping people reach their financial objectives, controlling risk, assisting in maintaining economic stability, lowering financial stress, and cultivating empathy and understanding. People can invest in knowledge about personal finance to create better financial futures for themselves and their communities.

The Value of Keeping a Budget and Monitoring Expenses

In order to achieve financial stability and long-term financial goals, budgeting and tracking expenses are essential personal finance activities. The following justifies the significance of tracking spending and creating a budget:

Financial Awareness: Keeping a budget and monitoring spending help people acquire a clear picture of their financial status. A budget and expense tracking help people understand their income, spending trends, and money management practices. Because of this understanding, people are able to find areas where they may reduce spending, save money, and make better financial decisions.

Budgeting assists people in identifying and prioritizing their financial objectives. Budgeting enables people to direct their money toward particular goals, such as building an emergency fund, paying off debt, or saving for a trip. By keeping track of their spending, people may keep an eye on how well they're doing in reaching their objectives and change as necessary to stay on course.

Financial Planning: Financial planning, both short- and long-term, is made easier by tracking spending and creating a budget. A budget helps people plan for both monthly and one-time expenses, such as gifts for the holidays or automobile maintenance, as well as recurrent costs like rent, utilities, and groceries. By keeping track of spending, people can prepare for future expenses and lessen the chance of financial emergencies or surprises.

Debt management: To properly manage debt, budgeting and spending tracking are critical. People can set aside money for debt repayment in an organized and controlled way by being aware of their cash flow and spending patterns. By keeping track of their spending, people can find ways to cut back on discretionary spending and put more money toward paying off debt, which will hasten the process of being debt-free.

Financial Security: By assisting people in living within their means and preventing overspending, budgeting and expense tracking help people maintain financial security. A budget that is in line with one's income and financial objectives helps people stay out of debt and create a safety net for unforeseen costs or crises. By keeping track of their spending, people may make sure they stick to their spending limits and practice financial restraint over time.

Better Decision Making: Keeping a budget and monitoring spending help people make more financially responsible choices. People who have a thorough grasp of their income and expenses are better able to prioritize their spending according to their beliefs and objectives and assess the financial effects of various decisions. This assists people in avoiding rash or pointless purchases and in making decisions that are in line with their long-term financial well-being.

Financial Freedom: Achieving financial independence and freedom requires careful planning and monitoring of spending. People can increase their financial stability and flexibility by building savings, investments, and passive income sources through prudent money management and living below their means. The foundation for reaching financial independence and leading a more contented and stress-free life is laid by creating a budget and monitoring your spending.

financial literacy, goal-setting, financial planning, debt management, financial security, better decision-making, and eventually financial freedom are all facilitated by budgeting and tracking spending. People may take charge of their finances, accomplish their goals, and create a better financial future for themselves and their family by adopting these behaviors into their daily financial routines.

Knowing the fundamentals of creating a budget

In order to successfully manage your finances and reach your financial objectives, it is imperative that you comprehend the fundamentals of budgeting. The essential elements of budgeting are broken down as follows:

Income: Figuring out your entire monthly income is the first step in making a budget. This covers all forms of revenue, including commissions, tips, bonuses, salaries, wages, and rental income, among others. Your income is the starting point for your budget since it tells you how much money you have left over for savings, expenses, and other financial objectives.

Expenses: The next step is to list and group your costs. Expenses are classified as variable or variable-bearing (e.g., groceries, dining out, entertainment, shopping) and fixed (e.g., rent or mortgage, utilities, insurance premiums), which are comparatively constant from month to month. It is crucial to monitor both regular and one-time costs in order to obtain a complete understanding of your spending patterns.

Savings and Financial Objectives: Set aside a certain percentage of your earnings for savings and financial objectives. This could be accumulating money for an emergency fund, paying off debt, setting aside money for a large purchase (like a house or car), or making investments for the future. Establish SMART goals specific, measurable, realistic, relevant, and time-bound to direct your savings efforts and monitor your advancement over time.

Select the budgeting technique that best suits your interests and financial circumstances. The zero-based budget, which allots every dollar of income to debt repayment, savings, or expenses; the 50/30/20 budget, which divides income into three categories needs, wants, and savings and debt repayment as well as the envelope system, which divides cash into different categories and puts it in envelopes to keep spending under control.

Tracking and Monitoring: To make sure you're remaining on track, keep a close eye on your expenditures and periodically check your budget. Record your income and expenses and compare them to the amounts you have allocated using spreadsheets, apps, or pen and paper. If your income, expenses, or financial objectives change, make the necessary adjustments to your budget.

Evaluate and Modify: Continually review your budget and make any required modifications. Changes in your goals for money, your expenses, or your income may necessitate making adjustments to your budget. When it comes to modifying your budget to align with your current priorities and financial status, exercise flexibility and initiative.

Building an emergency fund should be your first priority if you need to pay for unforeseen costs or financial problems. Save as much as possible in a high-yield savings account or other easily accessible, liquid account to cover three to six months' worth of living costs. In difficult times, having an emergency fund in place can bring financial security and peace of mind.

You may take charge of your finances, manage your money more skillfully, and work toward reaching your financial objectives by comprehending and putting these budgeting fundamentals into practice. To achieve long-term financial success, keep in mind that budgeting is a dynamic process that calls for constant attention and adjustment. Be proactive and involved in budget management.

The advantages of planning for freedom and stability in finances

Many advantages of budgeting support financial freedom and stability. The following are some of the main benefits:

Financial Awareness: Creating a budget helps you become more conscious of your earnings and outlays. You may get a comprehensive picture of your financial status by keeping track of your income and expenses. This knowledge enables you to prioritize your spending according to your financial objectives and make wise judgments on your spending patterns.

Control Over Spending: By setting boundaries and spending caps for your costs, a budget helps you keep tabs on how much you spend. You're less likely to overpay or make impulsive purchases when you have a budget in place. Alternatively, you can deliberately distribute your income to meet your needs, desires, and savings objectives.

Debt management: Creating a budget is a useful strategy for controlling and lowering debt. You can gradually get rid of debt by setting aside a certain percentage of your monthly income for debt repayment.

CHAPTER TWO

A budget enables you to pay off debt in order of priority and prevents you from taking on new debt, which eventually improves your financial stability and health.

Savings and Emergency Fund: Using a budget enables you to set aside money for emergencies first. By allocating a portion of your monthly salary to savings, you can build up money for unforeseen costs and future ambitions. An emergency fund acts as a safety net to shield you from financial ruin in the event of an unexpected medical bill, job loss, or other disaster.

Achieving Your Financial Goals: Creating a budget aids in goal setting and achievement. A budget offers a path to achieving your objectives, whether they are related to retirement, a new home, a trip, or other milestones. You can gradually move closer to realizing your goals by dissecting more ambitious goals into more doable chunks.

Decreased Financial tension: Having a budget in place helps to ease worry and tension related to money. You feel more assured and in charge of your finances when you have a well-thought-out plan for handling your money and reaching your objectives. Having a budget increases your sense of wellbeing and peace of mind by assisting you in anticipating costs, averting surprises, and planning for the future.

Better Financial Decision-Making: Budgeting promotes careful and methodical financial choices. Using a budget as a guide, you may assess the costs and benefits of various possibilities and set spending priorities according to your priorities and values. Making educated judgments about your spending, saving, and investing through budgeting will improve your results and increase your financial success.

Financial Stability and Freedom: In the end, budgeting prepares the path for both. You may attain your goals, accumulate wealth, and have more financial flexibility and independence by managing your money wisely and living within your means. By creating a budget, you can take charge of your money and give yourself and your family a better, more secure future.

creating a budget has several advantages that support financial independence and stability. Budgeting assists you in laying a strong basis for long-term financial success and well-being by raising financial awareness, lowering stress, managing debt, prioritizing savings, reaching goals, and eventually becoming financially independent.

Establishing and Preserving Good Credit

Achieving financial stability and getting access to opportunities like credit cards, loans, and low interest rates require building and keeping strong credit. To assist you in establishing and preserving good credit, follow these steps:

Recognize Credit Scores: Become acquainted with credit scores and their computation. Your credit score is a number that indicates how creditworthy you are; it is determined by a number of variables, including the duration of your credit history, the types of credit accounts you have, your payment history, your credit utilization, and recent credit inquiries. To be eligible for the best credit terms and offers, aim for a high credit score, usually over 700.

Pay Your Bills on Time: Your payment history has a significant impact on your credit score. Make sure to pay all of your bills on time, including those related to credit cards, loans, rent, utilities, and other expenses. Your credit score can be severely impacted by late payments, which can also make it more difficult for you to get credit in the future.

Control Credit Utilization: Use a minimal amount of your available credit to maintain a low credit utilization ratio. Maintain your credit card balances well below the credit limits ideally, no more than 30% of available credit. A high credit use rate may be a sign of financial strain and could lower your credit score.

Use Credit Responsibly: Make sure you only borrow money that you can afford to pay back while using credit. Steer clear of charging your credit cards to the limit or taking on more debt than you can handle. Use credit cards for ease of use and to establish credit, but make sure to pay off the entire amount each month to prevent interest fees and debt building.

Diversify Your Credit Types: Having a variety of credit kinds will help your credit score. This covers revolving credit accounts, like credit cards and credit lines, and installment loans, such mortgages and vehicle loans. Your creditworthiness might gradually increase if you show that you can manage your various forms of credit responsibly.

Monitor Your Credit Report: To guarantee accuracy and spot any mistakes or fraudulent activity, periodically check your credit report from each of the three major credit bureaus TransUnion, Equifax, and Experian. Every 12 months, you can obtain a free credit report from each bureau by visiting AnnualCreditReport.com. Keeping an eye on your credit report enables you to identify and resolve problems that can lower your credit score.

Limit Credit Applications: Try not to apply for too many credit cards at once, especially in a short amount of time. A hard inquiry is usually made on your credit record as a result of each credit application, which may temporarily reduce your credit score. Applying for new credit should be done carefully; only apply for credit accounts that you actually need or are eligible for.

Build Credit History: Get credit as early as feasible because it takes time to establish a good credit history. Applying for a secured credit card, adding yourself as an authorized user on someone else's credit card, or taking out a credit-builder loan can all help you create credit if you don't have much credit history or are new to the credit world.

Talk to Your Creditors: Be proactive in your communication with your creditors if you're having financial troubles or expect to have problems paying payments. In order to assist debtors in managing their debt and preventing adverse effects on their credit reports, some creditors provide hardship programs or alternative payment arrangements.

Be Patient and Persistent: Establishing and preserving good credit is a long-term process that calls for perseverance. Make consistent, prudent financial decisions your main priority, and track your development over time. You may establish a strong credit history and take advantage of having good credit for many years to come with commitment and hard work.

You can establish and preserve good credit by adhering to these guidelines and managing your credit responsibly. Good credit is necessary for reaching your financial objectives and taking advantage of future chances for increased financial flexibility.

Credit scores are numerical depictions of a person's creditworthiness that give lenders an idea of how likely it is that a borrower will make timely loan repayments. They have a big say in what interest rates and conditions people get on loans, credit cards, mortgages, and other types of credit, as well as whether or not they qualify for them. The meaning of credit scores is explained as follows:

Calculation: To determine a person's credit score, a number of elements pertaining to their credit history are analyzed using mathematical algorithms. The Fair Isaac Corporation created the FICO Score, which has a range of 300 to

850, and it is the most widely used credit scoring model. Similar scales are also used by other scoring algorithms, such VantageScore.

Factors: Credit scores are determined by a number of important variables, such as:

Payment History: The promptness with which credit accounts, such as credit cards, loans, and mortgages, have been paid off.

Credit utilization is the percentage of total credit limits that are being used, usually as a measure of how much credit is available.

Length of Credit History: The age of credit accounts, includes the average age of all accounts and the duration of time they have been open.

Credit Types: A combination of credit accounts, such as credit cards, revolving accounts, and installment loans (such as mortgages and vehicle loans).

The quantity of recent applications for new credit accounts and credit inquiries.

Significance: There are various reasons why credit ratings are important.

Loan Approval: Credit scores are used by lenders to determine how risky it is to lend to borrowers. People with higher credit ratings are more likely to be approved for credit cards and loans since they reflect lesser risk.

Interest Rates: Borrowers' interest rates on credit products are influenced by their credit scores as well. Higher credit score holders are usually eligible for reduced interest rates, which eventually translate into lower borrowing expenses.

Credit Limits: Lenders' credit limits may be influenced by a borrower's credit score. Higher credit limits may be granted to those with better credit scores, giving them more financial flexibility.

Employment and Housing: When recruiting new employees or renting out properties, certain businesses and landlords may also take credit scores into account. Although credit scores are not the only thing taken into account, they can be a good indicator of someone's dependability and sense of financial responsibility.

Monitoring and Improvement: People must always keep an eye on their credit scores and take action to raise them if needed. This can entail making on-time bill payments, lowering credit card debt, refraining from creating several new accounts quickly, and checking credit reports for mistakes or inconsistencies.

Credit scores are important financial indicators that affect people's borrowing costs, credit availability, and other elements of their financial lives. Through comprehension of credit ratings and proactive measures to uphold or enhance them, people can enhance their financial prospects and accomplish their objectives.

Putting Money Towards The Future

Building wealth and accomplishing long-term financial objectives require investing for the future. When making investments for the future, keep the following considerations in mind:

Start Early: When it comes to investing, time is one of the most important resources. Your investments have more time to develop and compound if you start investing early. Thanks to compound interest, even modest regular investments can grow into substantial wealth over time.

Establish Clear Goals: Prior to making any investments, you should clearly define your financial aims and objectives. Whether your savings are for your kids' school, your own retirement, a down payment on a house, or other long-term goals, establishing specific goals will help you allocate your assets and develop an investing plan.

Recognize Your Risk Tolerance: To find the best investment plan for you, evaluate your investment preferences and risk tolerance. Think about things like your time horizon, your financial objectives, and how comfortable you are with market volatility. Generally speaking, investments with larger potential returns also carry larger risk.

Diversify Your Portfolio: Managing risk and optimizing returns require diversification. Invest in a variety of businesses, asset classes, and geographical areas to lessen the impact of market swings on your portfolio. Long-term performance can be improved and volatility reduced with the use of diversification.

Invest Often: Regardless of market conditions, take advantage of dollar-cost averaging by making regular investments. You can potentially reduce your average cost per share over time by investing a set amount of money at regular intervals. This will allow you to purchase more shares during periods of low price and fewer shares during periods of high price.

Remain Up to Date: Remain up to date on developments in the financial markets, the economy, and investment opportunities. Stay informed on changes in investing regulations, market trends, and economic factors that could impact your portfolio. To assist you in making wise judgments, think about consulting financial consultants or investment specialists.

Monitor and Rebalance: Make sure your investment portfolio is consistently in line with your objectives and risk tolerance by reviewing it on a regular basis and making adjustments as necessary. Periodically rebalance your portfolio to keep the appropriate risk profile and asset allocation. If you want to take advantage of possibilities, think about adding new assets or selling old ones that don't meet your goals.

Invest for the Long Term: A long-term outlook is necessary when making investments for the future. Do not try to time the market or make rash judgments based on transient market swings. Rather, concentrate on a methodical buy-and-hold strategy that prioritizes endurance, constancy, and being invested across market cycles.

Think About Tax Efficiency: To reduce your tax liability, consider the tax ramifications of your investment choices and look into tax-efficient investment techniques. To optimize your investment returns and maximize tax benefits, make use of tax-advantaged accounts like Health Savings Accounts (HSAs), Individual Retirement Accounts (IRAs), and 401(k)s.

Remain Disciplined: Long-term financial goals and discipline are prerequisites for investing for the future.

CHAPTER THREE

Even in times of uncertainty, try not to let your emotions get in the way of your investing strategy and stay true to it. To succeed in investing over the long run, stay committed to your goals and keep a disciplined attitude.

You can make wise investments for the future, work toward reaching your financial objectives, and gradually accumulate wealth by adhering to these ideas and methods. Recall that investing entails dangers, therefore in order to make wise selections, you must do extensive study and consult a professional when necessary.

Investments and their long-term advantages

Several long-term advantages of investing can have a big influence on your financial situation in the future. Here are a few main benefits:

Wealth accumulation: By generating returns on your initial investment, investing enables you to increase your wealth over time. There is more room for growth when you invest in stocks, bonds, real estate, and other assets than when you just put money in a bank account.

Compound interest: Albert Einstein frequently refers to this as the "eighth wonder of the world". The idea of compound interest is that you can increase exponentially over time by earning interest on your interest. Your money has more time to multiply the earlier you start investing, which could eventually result in significant gains.

Financial freedom: You can strive toward financial independence by making long-term investments on a regular basis. This entails generating enough passive income from your investments to pay your bills and provide you additional flexibility and freedom in your life.

Diversification: Spreading your risk and lessening the effect of market swings on your portfolio are two benefits of investing in a range of assets. Over time, diversification can increase overall returns while safeguarding your investments.

Beat inflation: Over time, inflation reduces the buying power of your money. Investing in assets like stocks or real estate, which have a history of outpacing inflation, can help you maintain and possibly grow your purchasing power over time.

Retirement planning: Creating a retirement fund requires investing. Regular contributions to retirement accounts, such as IRAs or 401(k)s, allow you to secure a comfortable retirement lifestyle while also benefiting from tax advantages.

Planning for the future: You can leave a lasting legacy for your loved ones by investing. You can leave your financial resources to the next generation, giving them chances and financial security, by building money and assets over time.

Emotional restraint: Both emotional restraint and discipline are necessary for successful investing. Acquiring the ability to endure market fluctuations and maintaining a long-term investment plan will enable you to form crucial financial habits that you can carry into other aspects of your life.

Education and personal development: Investing offers a chance to pick up knowledge about economics, business operations, and financial markets. It can also promote financial literacy and personal development by imparting important lessons on risk management, patience, and decision-making.

All things considered, investment is an effective strategy for increasing wealth, reaching financial objectives, and long-term financial security. To maximize the rewards of investing, it's critical to get started early, maintain discipline, and, when necessary, seek advice from financial professionals.

Investment choices that are appropriate for college students

Investing can be an excellent method for college students to begin learning about financial markets and accumulating wealth. The following investing alternatives are appropriate for college students:

Stocks: College students can own a portion of firms they support by investing in individual stocks. Even though it's crucial to learn about and comprehend the businesses before making an investment, stocks have the potential to yield large profits in the long run.

Exchange-Traded Funds (ETFs): Like stocks, ETFs are investment funds that are traded on stock exchanges. By retaining a variety of assets, including stocks, bonds, and commodities, they provide diversification. ETFs are a well-liked option for novice investors because of their affordability and ease of use.

Mutual funds: These investment vehicles combine the capital of several individuals to purchase a variety of stocks, bonds, and other assets. They are a practical choice for college students who would rather take a hands-off approach to investing because they are overseen by experienced fund managers.

Robo-advisors: Robo-advisors are automated investment systems that build and manage diverse portfolios according to the objectives, time horizon, and risk tolerance of the investor using algorithms. They are perfect for college students with little income because they usually have low fees and no minimum investment requirements.

Index funds use identical equities in the same ratios as the index to track a certain market index, such the S&P 500. They are a well-liked option for passive investors since they provide cheap costs and wide market exposure.

Retirement Accounts: College students can begin saving for retirement by establishing an Individual Retirement Account (IRA) or, if one is offered by their employer, making contributions to a 401(k) or other workplace retirement plan. Over time, these accounts can assist students in accumulating a sizeable savings account and provide tax benefits.

Savings Accounts: Although savings accounts aren't considered investments, they provide a secure location to hold short-term or emergency savings. To get the most out of your funds, look for high-yield accounts with competitive interest rates.

Peer-to-peer Lending: Through these platforms, anyone can lend money to others and receive interest payments. Peer-to-peer lending can yield larger returns than traditional bonds or savings accounts, despite the associated risks.

Real estate crowdfunding: Platforms for real estate crowdfunding enable investors to pool their funds and make investments in residential and commercial real estate projects. Real estate exposure can be obtained with this option without requiring significant funds or active management.

Prioritizing their education, paying off high-interest debt, and creating an emergency fund should come before investing for college students. It's also critical to evaluate your risk tolerance, learn about and comprehend each investment option, and, if necessary, think about seeing a financial counselor for advice.

The significance of knowing your risk tolerance and beginning to invest early

Developing an effective investing strategy requires knowing your risk tolerance and getting started with investments early. This is the reason why:

The Value of Investing at an Early Age:

Power of Compounding: Your money has more time to increase through the power of compounding the earlier you start investing. Your investment returns can compound over time to produce further returns, resulting in exponential growth.

Potential for Long-Term Growth: Investing early enables you to benefit from financial markets prospects for long-term growth. Over longer investing horizons, stocks and other growth-oriented assets have historically yielded larger returns.

Ability to Weather Market Volatility: Investing early allows you to recover more quickly from brief setbacks and weather market downturns. Long-term investing allows you to ride out market turbulence and take advantage of the markets' general upward tendency.

Establishing Financial Discipline: Early investing promotes sound saving practices and financial discipline. It teaches the value of putting long-term objectives first and regularly allocating funds for investments, laying the groundwork for future financial success.

Restitution for Errors: By getting started early, you can afford to make investment mistakes and learn from them without suffering dire repercussions. You have more time to bounce back from setbacks and modify your investing plan in light of your learnings.

Comprehending Risk Tolerance

Aligning Investments with Goals: By being aware of your level of risk tolerance, you may better match your investing decisions to your time horizon and financial objectives. Your risk tolerance dictates which investments are appropriate for you as different investments have different levels of risk.

Avoiding Emotional Decisions: Being aware of your risk tolerance will help you avoid acting rashly or out of greed while making financial decisions. You're less prone to panic during market downturns or pursue speculative investments if you stick to your comfort zone.

Building a Balanced Portfolio: You may create a diversified investment portfolio that strikes a balance between risk and possible rewards by having a clear grasp of your risk tolerance. A variety of assets, including stocks, bonds, and cash equivalents, might be included in your portfolio based on your investing goals and risk tolerance.

Investing for the Long Term: Investors that have a high risk tolerance are more likely to stick with growth-oriented investments, which could result in longer-term gains. To protect capital and reduce volatility, investors with a lower risk tolerance might, on the other hand, favor more conservative choices.

Periodic Review and Adjustment: A number of factors, including age, financial situation, and market conditions, can affect your risk tolerance over time. To make sure your investing plan stays in line with your objectives and tastes, it's critical to regularly reevaluate your risk tolerance and make the necessary adjustments.

All things considered, the first stages to accumulating wealth and attaining financial success are beginning to invest early and determining your level of risk tolerance. You may optimize the advantages of long-term investing while reducing needless stress and uncertainty by being proactive in your investing and adhering to your risk tolerance.

Summary

In conclusion, learning the foundations of personal finance in college can have a significant influence on your success in the future and financial well-being. You may make educated judgments, steer clear of typical mistakes, and position yourself for long-term financial independence and stability by understanding important concepts and practices early on. By considering the three key concepts in personal finance that many college students wish they had learned, such budgeting, creditworthiness, and investing for the future, you can be proactive in managing your finances, forming sound financial habits, and reaching your financial objectives. You may overcome life's financial obstacles with confidence and prosper in the years to come if you keep learning, adapting, and prioritizing your financial health. Keep in mind that financial education is a lifelong effort.

THE END